VICTORY IN EUROPE

FROM D-DAY TO VE-DAY IN PICTURES

CHANCELLOR
PRESS

Acknowledgements

Text by Chris Bishop
Design and maps by Louise Griffiths

The publishers would like to thank the following
organizations for their kind permission to reproduce the
photographs in this book:

Hulton Deutsch Collection: front and back cover
photographs, 1, 11, 12, 13, 14, 15, 16, 17, 18, 19, 20, 21,
22, 23, 24, 25, 31, 32, 33, 34, 35, 36, 37, 38, 39, 40, 41,
43, 44, 45, 46, 47, 56, 57, 66, 75, 76, 77, 78, 79, 80, 81,
82, 88, 92, 93, 99, 100, 101, 102, 103, 106, 108, 109, 110,
112; The Trustees of the Imperial War Museum, London:
42, 83; Novosti (London): 53, 54, 55, 58, 59, 60, 61, 62,
63, 64, 65, 67, 68, 69, 84, 85, 86, 87, 89, 90, 91, 94, 95,
104; Popperfoto: 111; reproduced by permission of
Punch: 6, 26, 48, 70, 96; RangePictures/Bettmann
Archive, New York Daily Mirror Collection 105,
UPI/Harold Siegman 107.

First published in Great Britain in 1995
by Chancellor Press, an imprint of
Reed Consumer Books Limited
Michelin House, 81 Fulham Road, London SW3 6RB
and Auckland, Melbourne, Singapore and Toronto

Copyright © 1995 Reed International Books Limited

ISBN 1 85152 877 6

A catalogue record for this book is available from the
British Library

Produced by Mandarin Offset, Hong Kong
Printed in Hong Kong

Contents

Chronology

6 June 1944	D-Day: Allies land more than 150,000 men on the beaches of Normandy in France.	**12 September**	US 1st Army crosses German border near Aachen.	**28 March**	Red Army units reach Austrian border.

6 June 1944 — D-Day: Allies land more than 150,000 men on the beaches of Normandy in France.

13 June — The first of the V1 flying bombs hit England.

22 June — Russians launch their summer offensive on the Eastern Front.

9 July — British liberate Caen.

17 July — Russian Army enters Poland.

20 July — July Bomb Plot. Several of Hitler's generals attempt to assassinate him. The bomb explodes but Hitler survives.

24 July — Allies begin the breakout from the Normandy beach-head.

26 July — Russians reach river Vistula in Poland.

27 July — US forces breakthrough west of St Lô. Russians capture Lvov.

28 July — Red Army takes Brest-Litovsk and Premysl.

1 August — Warsaw Rising. General Patton takes command of US 3rd Army.

4 August — US 3rd Army takes Rennes.

6 August — US 3rd Army reaches outskirts of Brest.

13 August — Germans begin withdrawal through Falaise Gap.

14 August — Red Army launches offensive from Vistula bridgehead.

19 August — Patton's forces reach Seine on each side of Paris.

23 August — Coup d'état in Romania. Marshal Antonescu overthrown.

25 August — Allied forces led by General Leclerc's French 2nd Armoured Division liberate Paris.

31 August — Montgomery promoted to Field Marshal.

3 September — British 2nd Army liberates Brussels.

4 September — British 2nd Army reaches Antwerp.

6 September — Russians reach Yugoslav border.

8 September — First V2 rocket attack on London. Red Army drives unopposed into Bulgaria.

12 September — US 1st Army crosses German border near Aachen.

15 September — US 1st Army breaks through Siegfried Line.

17 September — Operation 'Market Garden'; Allied 1st Airborne Army drop at Eindhoven, Nijmegen and Arnhem.

19 September — British Paratroops at Arnhem Bridge cut off. US and British troops meet at Nijmegen.

20 September — Bridges at Nijmegen secured by Allies.

26 September — Last survivors of Arnhem battle withdraw.

1 October — Red Army enters Yugoslavia.

2 October — Polish Home Army surrenders in Warsaw.

16 October — Hungary asks for Armistice. Admiral Horthy kidnapped by SS Commando Otto Skorzeny.

7 November — Roosevelt elected President for fourth term.

24 November — French troops take Strasbourg.

29 November — Russians cross Danube.

16 December — Beginning of the Battle of the Bulge.

21 December — US 101st Airborne Division besieged in Bastogne.

26 December — US 3rd Army tanks drive up to relieve Bastogne.

27 December — Red Army completes encirclement of Budapest.

12 January — Russians launch Winter Offensive in south.

17 January — Warsaw liberated by Polish troops attached to Red Army.

19 January — Russians capture Cracow.

5 February — British and Canadian drive to the Rhine begins.

11 February — German garrison in Budapest destroyed.

26 February — Canadian units drive into Holland.

7 March — US 1st Army crosses Remagen bridge over Rhine.

23 March — British and Canadians launch offensive across Rhine.

24 March — British and US airborne forces dropped at Wesel and link up with British and Canadians.

28 March — Red Army units reach Austrian border.

29 March — US 3rd Army reaches Frankfurt.

30 March — Russians occupy Danzig.

9 April — Russians storm Koenigsberg Fortress.

10 April — US 9th Army reaches Hannover.

12 April — Death of President Roosevelt; Vice-President Truman takes office.

13 April — Vienna occupied by Red Army. British and Americans reach Belsen and Buchenwald concentration camps.

16 April — Red Army drive on Berlin opens.

18 April — US 3rd Army reaches Czechoslovakia. 9th Army takes Magdeberg.

19 April — US 1st Army moves into Leipzig.

20 April — US 7th Army reaches Nuremberg.

21 April — Red Army drives each side of Berlin. Soviet 8th Army in south-east suburbs. French troops enter Stuttgart.

23 April — Zhukov's and Koniev's forces break into Berlin.

24 April — British and Canadians enter Bremen.

25 April — US and Red Army units meet at Torgau on the Elbe.

29 April — Hitler marries Eva Braun and appoints Admiral Doenitz as successor.

30 April — Hitler commits suicide.

2 May — Red Army occupies Berlin. Surrender of all German forces in Italy.

4 May — Montgomery receives surrender of German forces in Holland, Denmark and north-west Germany, effective 8 a.m.

7 May — In General Eisenhower's headquarters at Reims General Jodl signs instrument of surrender of all German forces.

8 May — VE-Day. German surrender to Russians signed at Karlshorst, near Berlin.

Preface

The Second World War was the bitterest conflict in human history. It began as a series of local confrontations and grew into a struggle for global mastery, fought on three continents and five oceans, which was ultimately settled by the use of nuclear weapons. A total of 60 million people died throughout the world, and the impact of this trauma on subsequent generations has yet to become clear.

But at the point at which our story begins, the war has not yet been won. Germany, still smarting from defeat in the Great War and breaking free from the constraints of the Treaty of Versailles, had come under the spell of Adolf Hitler and the Nazi Party. Their aim was to establish hegemony in Europe, an aim which was opposed by Britain and France. The first shots were fired in the invasion of Poland in 1939, but for the months of the 'Phoney War' all the western powers could do was prepare for the fighting they knew would come.

When Germany did attack, it was to stunning effect. France was over-run, and British forces were driven off the continent. Only the RAF's victory in the Battle of Britain prevented Britain from falling under Nazi domination. The situation was desperate, however: the U-boat menace endangered the nation's sea-borne lifeline, and Italy's declaration of war threatened to cut the vital Mediterranean links with the Empire.

Then Hitler attacked Russia in June 1941, and now it was the Germans who were faced with a two-front war. Despite devastating early successes, when huge territorial gains were made with lightning speed and millions of Soviet soldiers were killed or captured, by Christmas the Wehrmacht had ground to a halt in front of Moscow. And the huge resources of the Soviet Union were just coming into play. The turning point came in December of that year, although few would have recognised it at the time. Hitler's ally, Japan, attacked Pearl Harbor and almost immediately Germany declared war on the United States. Now the immense wealth and industrial muscle of the world's mightiest economy was placed solidly behind the Allied cause.

By the middle of 1942, the Axis powers were at their height. German armies were pushing towards the Caucasus mountains and the Volga, while the British had been driven back to the gates of Egypt. Japan had acquired a huge empire in the Pacific and South-East Asia.

However, during the last three months of 1942 the British won the battle of El Alamein in North Africa, Stalingrad was held in an epic defence, Allied troops landed in North-West Africa and preparations for the invasion of Italy began. In the Pacific the US Fleet had begun the island-hopping campaign which was to end in Tokyo Bay.

And as the Soviet army began to push the Nazis back in the east, there was only one more piece to be fitted into the jigsaw. At some stage, the Allies were going to have to take the war to the Germans on the continent of Europe. But where was the attack to happen? And when?

We begin our story with the D-Day landings in June 1944, which marked the beginning of the end.

ACCORDING TO PLAN

'... moreover, the longer they wait, the better our preparations.'

The Normandy Landings

In the spring of 1944 Hitler knew that the outcome of the war would be decided in France. In the east, the Red Army was growing in strength, while Germany simply did not have enough men to replace those that had been lost. Allied bombers were laying waste to German industry. Hundreds of thousands of troops were tied down in Italy. Another front on the western flank of Fortress Europe would almost certainly prove too much for the Germans, but if the Allied invasion of France were to fail the Wehrmacht would have a chance to concentrate on the Soviet threat. Any further Allied action in the west should be countered by the 'V' weapons which Germany expected soon, and it was hoped that they would batter Britain at least into submission.

The German high command was convinced that the Allied landings would take place in the Pas de Calais area. It was reasonably flat, there were good beaches and above all it was the closest part of France to Britain's major ports. Thanks to an exceptionally well orchestrated disinformation campaign, most German commanders continued to expect the main landings at Calais even after the Normandy landings had begun.

The exact timing of the Allied invasion depended on tides and the weather. The invasion needed to take place at dawn at low tide, which indicated either the middle of May or the beginning of June. General Dwight D. Eisenhower, the supreme Allied commander, ordered the attack for 5 June, but because of poor weather the assault was delayed for 24 hours until the 6th.

The invasion was spearheaded by a massive airborne assault. The American 82nd and 101st Airborne Divisions dropped by parachute and glider to seize vital ground inland of the western flank of the invasion beaches, while the British 6th Airborne Division was dropped on the eastern flank. The drop was chaotic, with both American divisions scattered over a wide area. Small groups of paratroopers coalesced and fought a series of confused actions, eventually taking the vital crossroads at St Mère Eglise. The British, charged with capturing the crossings over the river Orne and Caen Canal were more successful, and reached most objectives before dawn.

The main landings on five beaches began at 0630 on 6 June. Overall ground command was given to General Sir Bernard Montgomery, with General Omar N. Bradley in command of US forces. Preceded by a heavy air and naval bombardment, American troops swept ashore on 'Utah' beach. Although 2,000 metres from their intended landing points, they met only light opposition. Leading elements quickly began pushing inland to reach the American paratroops, while for the rest of the day the beach buzzed as men and supplies were brought ashore.

At 'Omaha' beach German opposition was determined, and a choppy sea made things worse. By nightfall the Americans were barely clinging to the beach, cut off from 'Utah' by flooded estuaries and from the British 'Gold' beach by the German-held fishing port of Port-en-Bessin. This was finally taken by the Royal Marines on 8 June. In the Allied centre the landings at 'Gold' beach faced similar problems with the surf, but opposition was lighter and by the afternoon the British 50th Division was heading inland. On 'Juno' beach the Canadians were 10 kilometres inland by the end of the day, although short of the very ambitious objectives set for them. The next day they had to fight off a savage counter-attack by the SS Panzer Division 'Hitler Jugend'. At 'Sword', the easternmost beach, the troops encountered many more obstacles than they had been led to expect, and they were the object of the only major German attack on D-Day – an unsuccessful thrust by the 21st Panzer Division, which attempted to split the British and Canadian forces.

Had the Wehrmacht deployed its armour on day one, the Allies might still have been pushed into the sea. But Hitler refused to allow the reserve to be moved until it was too late. By the end of D-Day over 156,000 troops had been landed in the greatest amphibious operation in the history of warfare, at a cost of 9,000 casualties. The next day co-ordinated Allied attacks linked the five invasion beaches to form an 80-kilometre front which no subsequent German attack seriously threatened to breach.

The success of those first, heady days was not to last. Over the next four weeks advances slowed and ground to a halt as German resistance stiffened. By the end of June there were a lot of worried faces in Whitehall and Washington. Men who had been planning the liberation of Europe for years now suspected that their plans were going dreadfully wrong.

But the man in charge of the troops on the ground was not one of them. General

Montgomery's unshakeable confidence heartened those who believed in him – and was a constant irritant to those who did not. As early as 11 June Montgomery had stated that his objective was to draw the bulk of the enemy on to the eastern end of the bridgehead, i.e. towards Dempsey's forces near Caen, thus lessening the opposition in front of the Americans. If the enemy were weakened enough, Bradley could break out across the Selune river just south of Avranches. Once the gap had been made, the recently formed US 3rd Army under the flamboyant Lieutenant General George Patton could be freed to take the whole of Brittany and the vital ports of Brest, Lorient and St Nazaire.

That is exactly what happened. The battle of attrition on the British sector sucked in more and more of the German reserves. The fighting was fierce, and the town of Caen was obliterated in the process, but two months after the landings the breakout seemed possible.

On 1 August Patton was let loose. His US 3rd Army, four corps containing eight infantry and four armoured divisions, was given the task of liberating Brittany and its vital ports as quickly as possible. Patton modified the plan. Middleton's VIII Corps was to liberate Brittany while the rest of the Army headed towards Chartres and Orleans, over 160 kilometres away. Beyond lay the Seine and Paris, and Patton was determined to reach the French capital. By 8 August Haislip's XV Corps was not only across the Mayenne but had reached Le Mans. Walker's XX Corps took Angers on 11 August and raced forward towards the Chartres/Orleans gap, moving at up to 30 kilometres per day.

But there now occurred a slight check to the onward rush. On 4 August four Panzer divisions of General Paul Hausser's 7th Army had advanced westwards through Mortain towards Avranches and were now on the attack. Bradley, by now commanding the 12th Army Group, sensed the danger and threw in two corps from the US 1st Army. It took some bitter fighting, but Hausser was thrown back. There were now two German armies and a Panzergruppe (nearly 100,000 men) concentrated south-west of Falaise. Dempsey's British and Canadians were a few miles north of Falaise and Haislip's tanks were at Le Mans. It needed no great imagination to see what would happen if they were to meet.

Poor liaison meant that the Falaise Gap was not closed with total effectiveness. Nevertheless, in the battle for the pocket the Germans lost some 60,000 men and a massive amount of equipment.

To the south Walker took Chartres by 16 August, and Eddy's XII Corps took Orleans. Patton's divisions were by now scattered across more than 400 kilometres of French soil, and the gap between them was to widen even further. Haislip's men left Dreux on the 16th and reached Mantes-Gassicourt three days later. Walker left Chartres on the same day and reached Melun and Fontainebleau on the 20th, cutting the Seine both above and below Paris almost simultaneously. In 21 days, therefore, Patton's 3rd Army had advanced 320 kilometres eastwards from Avranches to the Seine, and 240 kilometres westwards as far as Brest.

The next major prize was Paris.

D-Day and the Breakout

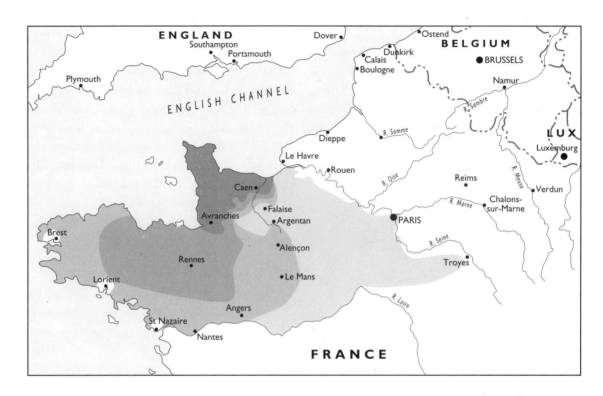

Key

Area conquered to 1 August

Area conquered to 6 August

Area conquered to 13 August

Area conquered to 25 August

Allied troops and supplies land on the Normandy
beaches

above US medics treat wounded soldiers after the
initial D-Day landings

right Moving away from the beaches, Allied
soldiers begin to push inland

The massive build-up of men and materials
continues

Some of the first German prisoners captured by the
Allies on French soil

above A direct hit: an American bazooka team knock out a German tank

right The battle for a village street in Normandy

left The historic town of Caen in ruins after the
attentions of Allied bombers and the liberating
armies

above Some of the thousands of prisoners captured
as the German army begins to disintegrate

below French children search among abandoned
German vehicles for looted goods

right Exhausted by the speed of the advance
towards the Seine, a British soldier catches up on
some sleep

above American soldiers pay their last respects at
the graves of their dead colleagues near St Mère
Eglise

right French villagers welcome their liberators

x

below A GI tries to explain to a French woman that
this road is closed to civilians

right Two French children give General Patton
their views on the progress of the war

THE NEW GATEWAY

From the Seine to the Rhine

The late summer of 1944 was marked by a series of rapid advances through the remnants of the German armed forces in France. The arrival of the Allied armies on the Seine only 80 days after D-Day was undoubtedly a cause for celebration and congratulation for the troops and their commanders. But the advance had been so fast that it was a matter of concern for those charged with the mundane business of keeping the men supplied with food and ammunition, and – even more crucial and difficult – the vehicles with fuel.

Cherbourg, though in Allied hands, was still not fully operational because of the damage and sabotage it had suffered before capture, one Mulberry harbour was wrecked and the other half-operational, and the fact that the Germans had fought so hard during the early weeks had constricted the size of the bridgehead in which the original stores dumps had been formed. The British had now wrenched themselves away from Caen and the Falaise area and the Americans were 350 kilometres away past Fontainebleau.

Montgomery felt that both Army Groups – his own 21st and General Bradley's 12th – should together drive north-eastwards into Belgium as a solid mass, so strong that it need fear nothing, then divide shortly before they both crossed the Rhine with the British and Canadians sweeping along the northern edge of the Ruhr to meet the Americans who would have taken the southern route on the far side. However, there was great pressure on General Eisenhower, who by now had taken overall command of the land forces from Montgomery, to stick to the original pre-D-Day concept of a 'broad front' advance across France which would make the fullest use of the excellent road system in western Europe, and this view prevailed.

But first there was Paris. From a military viewpoint the capital city was not an important strategic objective, and liberating it would mean syphoning off thousands of tons of fuel, ammunition and other essential supplies desperately needed by the Allied armies. Political considerations dictated otherwise, however, and Eisenhower eventually gave the order that the city should be liberated as soon as possible, with the French 2nd Armoured Division in the van. On 25 August French and US troops drove into Paris to a tumultuous reception.

While Paris was in the process of liberation, the bulk of the Allied armies was crossing the Seine. The day after the US 4th Division arrived in the French capital, Hodges' 1st Army began a drive towards Aachen and the Ardennes. Further south, Patton's 3rd Army reached Reims, Verdun and Commercy in an exhilarating chase punctuated by short and vicious bursts of fighting. The British were moving equally fast. The Guards reached Brussels, suffering their greatest delays as the liberated inhabitants celebrated. But although Antwerp was taken the next day, positions dominating its vast complex of quays and wharves had been strongly occupied by the

Germans. It would be three months before the last defenders were cleared and the port could be used.

Montgomery now proposed using the Allied 1st Airborne Army to form 'an airborne carpet' along a corridor 100 kilometres long from the border to cross the Rhine, taking and holding the bridges at Eindhoven, Nijmegen and Arnhem. Dempsey's and Hodges' armies would then stream across to reach the north German plain. Supported by the rest of the Allied armies, they would drive straight for Berlin.

During the morning of Sunday, 17 September 1944, the greatest airborne armada of all time took to the air. The smaller stream carried the men of the US 101st Airborne Division to their drop zone at Eindhoven. The larger part carried the US 82nd Airborne Division east towards the area between Grave and Nijmegen, and carried elements of the British 1st Airborne Division towards the town of Arnhem and its vital bridge of the Neder Rijn. The bridge at Arnhem was the tip of Operation 'Market Garden'. Although the landing there went well, troop movements were slow to begin. Radio communications were difficult – in those pre-transistor days, no satisfactory small portable set had yet been manufactured. But there was an even bigger problem: the Arnhem area was being used for recuperation by two crack SS Panzer divisions.

Throughout the next two days separate battles raged with ever-increasing ferocity, the advantage moving to the Germans as more and more Panzer troops were fed into the fighting. The outnumbered paratroopers needed the arrival of the 2nd Army, but the ground thrust had been delayed at Nijmegen by fierce German defences. The lightly-armed paratroopers had been told that they would be relieved within two or three days: they were on their own for eight. Allied troops at last reached the river on Sunday afternoon, and

the surviving exhausted, famished, desperate paratroops were evacuated the following night.

Operation 'Market Garden' had been a good idea. It was defeated by lack of information of enemy dispositions around Arnhem, by bad luck with the weather which had contributed to XXX Corps' delay, and by mistaken planning which had dropped 1st Airborne Division too far from its objective.

By mid-December 1944 the British and Canadians had at last cleared Antwerp for shipping, and two US armies were set to threaten the vital Roer dams. In the south General Patton's 3rd Army, after its spectacular drive across France, was aimed towards the Rhine at Mannheim. Between the two powerful groupings were strung out some 80,000 American troops along 140 kilometres of front. It was a quiet sector covering the Ardennes and facing the sparsely settled German Schnee Eifel. Few of the troops were experienced. Suddenly, on the morning of 16 December, began the heaviest artillery bombardment even the veterans among them had encountered. Within two hours, forward positions had been overrun by German shock troops, followed by powerful Panzer and Panzergrenadier units.

Even as the fighting in the Falaise Gap was ending in August, Hitler had been planning a counter-offensive in the west. A force of some 25 divisions had been scraped together, and some 200,000 men in three powerful armies would take part in Operation 'Wacht am Rhein'. They were equipped with more tanks, more artillery and more ammunition than any German force had seen for a year. The objective for this surreptitiously assembled force was Antwerp, together with the splitting of the Allied armies threatening the German frontier. The action was intended to provide an immense boost to the morale of the German public, together with such a shock to the

Allies that the consequent disarray would wreck their future strategic planning for weeks and possibly months.

Aided by that essential factor of surprise, leading elements of the 1st SS Panzer Division swept through a gap in American lines to Honsfeld in the north, captured a large petrol dump at Bullingen and then caught American troops on the move at Malmedy crossroads before racing on towards Stavelot. But the SS men, veterans of the no-quarter fighting on the Eastern Front, murdered nearly 200 American prisoners at Honsfeld, Bullingen and Malmedy. When rumour of the massacres reached the embattled American positions, it caused even the greenest units to fight with a committed ferocity which baulked the important German thrust to the south.

Another force to the south was held by the artillery and tank-destroyers of an American infantry division. The main drive was forced southwards into the gap between St Vith and the other vital road junction, Bastogne. And it was here that the attentions of both attackers and defenders became concentrated. General Bradley ordered General Hodges in the north to swing some of his 1st Army divisions back to hold a flank and then drive down to St Vith, and Patton to do the same in the south and send his crack 4th Armoured Division up to relieve Bastogne.

In the meantime, Eisenhower had released his reserves. The two Airborne Divisions, recently recovered from their battles at Nijmegen and Eindhoven, raced north from Patton's lines. The 101st Airborne reached Bastogne, where they were almost immediately surrounded and began a historic defence, and the 82nd Airborne went on to St Vith. Montgomery, by now promoted to Field Marshal, had taken command of the northern flank. The British 29th Armoured Brigade supported the American right flank to hold the deepest German penetration, and when the US 2nd Armoured Division arrived the next day Hitler's last offensive in the west – the so-called 'Battle of the Bulge' – was over.

It had given the Allies a shock and it would be weeks before the Ardennes salient was nipped off but, given the huge resources available to them, it proved nothing more than a delay. By contrast, the assault had used up most of Germany's remaining reserve of military material, and the manpower loss could not be made good.

By the New Year, the front line ran from the Scheldte Estuary past Nijmegen, across a narrow land-bridge to the Maas and south to the Roer and the Roer dams. It was time to regroup, re-supply and prepare for the final offensives into Germany: across the Rhine and into the heart of the Thousand-Year Reich.

The Advance to the Rhine

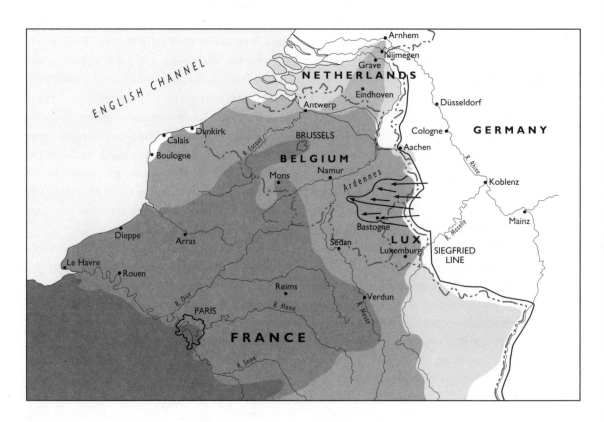

Key

- Area conquered to 25 August
- Area conquered to 3 September
- Area conquered to 15 September
- Area conquered to 30 September
- Area conquered to 16 December
- ← 'The Battle of the Bulge':
  German advance 16 – 25 December

Crowds cheer liberating troops entering Paris

On the barricades of Paris, members of the French
Resistance movement celebrate the liberation

Cheering crowds welcome American troops as they
approach one of the barricades erected by the
Resistance

above Soldiers of the Resistance forces entering
Paris, August 1944

right Members of the Resistance sheltering behind
trees keep watch for German snipers

above Fierce fighting took place around the
Chamber of Deputies, until a German officer
negotiated a surrender

right Members of the French Resistance clearing
German soldiers out of a Paris building

37

above A German officer bandages the wounds of another, as the staff of General Choltitz sit on the platform at Montparnasse station following the surrender of the Nazi Commander of Paris and 10,000 troops

right Guarded by the French police, German prisoners march through the streets of Paris on their way to a POW camp

left General de Gaulle heads the procession from
the Arc de Triomphe to the Place de la Concorde
during the celebrations marking the liberation of
Paris from Nazi control

above American troops march down the Champs
Elysées during the 'Victory' parade

left The people of Brussels give British and Belgian
troops a rapturous welcome

above American bombers drop supplies to Allied
paratroopers behind German lines in Holland

British Guards cheered into Eindhoven on their race
to link up with the airborne troops

Part of the amphibious fleet comprising assault
boats, 'Buffaloes' and 'Ducks' move into a flooded
Dutch village to rescue Allied troops

above In the snow-covered Ardennes, transport vehicles move up to the front with ammunition for the guns

right A dead German soldier lies on the road to Laroche in the Ardennes

JOE'S WAY

The Eastern Front

On 22 June 1944, three years to the day after Germany had launched Operation Barbarossa, the great Soviet summer offensive opened. Far to the west, Anglo-American armies were fighting in Normandy, but the bulk of the still formidable German Army was here in the east. But even they could not have expected the hurricane that was about to be unleashed. From Velikiye Luki in the north around a huge arc to Kovel below the Pripet Marshes, the artillery of four Red Army fronts – 15 armies – crashed out. While the aircraft of four air armies flew overhead, the Red Army moved out of its concentration areas into the attack. Units were at full strength and more, some infantry and tank units being 60 per cent over establishment.

Their objective was simple: to obliterate the German Army Group Centre. This immensely powerful force consisted of three infantry armies and one Panzer army, more than a million men with 1,000 of the best tanks in the world supported by 1,400 aircraft. Once this force had been smashed, the Soviet aim was to roll back the Finnish and German armies to the north, and the Hungarian, Romanian and German armies to the south.

Within a week the three main bastions of the German defences had been first cut off, then captured: Vitebsk in the north by converging attacks from General Bagramyan's 1st Baltic Front above and General Chernyakovsky's 3rd Belorussian Front below, Mogilev by General Zakharov's 2nd Belorussian Front, and Bobruisk by Marshal Rokossovsky's 1st Belorussian Front. Rokossovsky's troops had moved massively but secretly by night, attacking through marshes the Germans had considered impassable. Parts of two Panzer corps were cut off and bombed into disintegration before Bobruisk fell, yielding 24,000 prisoners.

By 4 July the Russians had driven forward nearly 240 kilometres, leaving only one pocket of German resistance behind, which surrendered on 11 July. The momentum never flagged. Everywhere the Germans were in full retreat, though they could still occasionally turn and strike back ferociously. In spite of the by no means negligible resistance, armies of the 1st Baltic Front forced the Dvina and took Polotsk within days. Chernyakovsky and Zakharov drove for Vilnius and Bialystok, taking the latter at the end of the month. Generaloberst Heinz Guderian, the great Panzer innovator who had been out of favour since 1941, had been recalled to take the poisoned chalice as Chief of the German General Staff. But it was far too late. Almost the first thing he did was to note caustically in his diary: 'Army Group Centre has now ceased to exist.'

To the north, Chernyakovsky's right flank drove through Lithuania and by the end of August had reached the borders of East Prussia. Brest-Litovsk fell to Rokossovsky on 28 July and soon afterwards his forces had reached the Bug river north of Warsaw. On his left General

Chuikov's 8th Guards Army had stormed out of Kovel, captured Lublin and reached the Vistula, which they crossed on 2 August. The Russians were also on the offensive further south. On 13 July Marshal Koniev's Ukrainian Front drove forwards, but met very strong resistance. It was not until two more tank armies had been brought up from reserve on the 16th that the tremendous weight of men and fire-power began to tell on the German Army Group North Ukraine.

On and on the Red Army pushed. Forty thousand Germans were surrounded near Brody, while Rokossovsky's right-hand army drove straight to the Vistula, crossing it to create a bridgehead at Sandomir. Lvov was flanked to the north, and a tank army captured the city on 27 July. Przemysl fell, then Mielec in the north and Nadvornaya in the south. By the end of August the Red Army was well into Poland, and was closing on the old Czech and Hungarian borders: in two months Soviet troops had advanced nearly 800 kilometres. Success had come at great cost, but the complete annihilation of the million-strong Army Group Centre made the cost worth while. Now the time had come again to pause and reorganize the supply lines for the next advance on this front.

One consequence of this inactivity was the tragedy of the Warsaw rising. With the Red Army all but at the gates of the city, the Polish Home Army and the Jewish ghetto rose up against the German occupiers. After weeks of fierce fighting, the rising was brutally put down and the ghetto razed by the SS. Only after it was all over did the Soviets move forward and take the city.

To the south, another campaign was about to open. Since the days of the Tsars, the Balkans have always been seen as areas of natural Russian interest, and Stalin held much the same views as his Romanov predecessors. On 20 August, Malinovsky's 2nd Ukrainian Front broke

through the defences of Army Group South Ukraine in the Pruth valley opposite Jassy, and by the 24th the German 6th Army had been surrounded. Its destruction seemed inevitable when politics intervened. A coup d'état took place in Bucharest. The pro-Nazi Marshal Antonescu was overthrown, King Michael took his place, and the government promptly sued for peace with the Allies. Two Romanian armies laid down their arms, and southern Bessarabia, the Danube delta and the Carpathian passes to the north lay open to the Soviet armies.

By the end of the month, Romania was in the process of being occupied by the Red Army, and Bulgaria to the south was about to be invaded by one of Tolbukhin's armies, driving down the Black Sea coast through Constanta. A pro-Allied group of officers now seized control in Bulgaria and welcomed the Red Army – so the invasion became 'a visit by friendly forces', who raced through Sofia on 15 September, collected two Bulgarian armies and pressed on to the Yugoslav border. By 8 September, Malinovsky's armies had joined Tolbukhin's, and on the 28th they moved forward together to link up with Marshal Tito's Partisans while the 46th Army of 2nd Ukrainian Front drove in over the Romanian border north of the Danube.

Two German Army Groups seemed to be in a trap. But Army Group F under General Weichs was holding open an escape corridor, and General Lohr's Army Group E, retreating up through Greece, was fighting so hard that it was 20 October before Belgrade was in Allied hands. There was no annihilation as there had been in the north: the bulk of both German army groups had raced through the gap to join a hastily forming defence line in Hungary, where yet another attempt to desert the Axis had been foiled. On 16 October Admiral Horthy, Hungary's dictator, declared a withdrawal from the pact with

Germany. He had never been an enthusiastic Fascist. However, before he could make contact with the Allies, he was kidnapped by the daring SS commando Otto Skorzeny.

German armies from Austria poured into Hungary, reinforced by troops pulled from Greece and Yugoslavia. By the time Malinovksy's and Tolbukhin's armies had assembled for a drive up from the Lake Balaton area, not only were the Germans present in force, but Budapest in particular was strongly held and fortified. In November, the Soviet armies were fighting their way north on each side of the Hungarian capital, slowly, implacably, but at great cost. On 25 December, when the city and its 180,000 defenders was finally surrounded, it was decided that there was no chance of taking it by storm. Budapest was besieged. Super-heavy artillery was called up from hundreds of miles back in the Soviet Union, extra divisions from reserves, supplies and food from wherever they could be found.

The final assault here, as in the north, must wait until 1945.

The Soviet Offensives, 1944

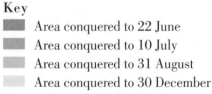

Key

- Area conquered to 22 June
- Area conquered to 10 July
- Area conquered to 31 August
- Area conquered to 30 December

right By 1944 the Soviet soldier was a battle-hardened veteran of the desperate fighting on the Eastern Front. Thirteen and a half million made the ultimate sacrifice in the struggle against Nazism

left The crew of a Soviet tank pause to check
directions during the battle for Czestochowa, Poland

below Soviet infantry storm the railway station
in Lvov

above After 63 days of bitter fighting in Warsaw,
German troops blindfold Countess Tarnowska,
President of the Polish Red Cross, as she arrives at
the German lines to discuss the surrender terms of
the exhausted Poles

right After the collapse of the Warsaw rising an
old couple, surrounded by SS officers, are issued
with soup

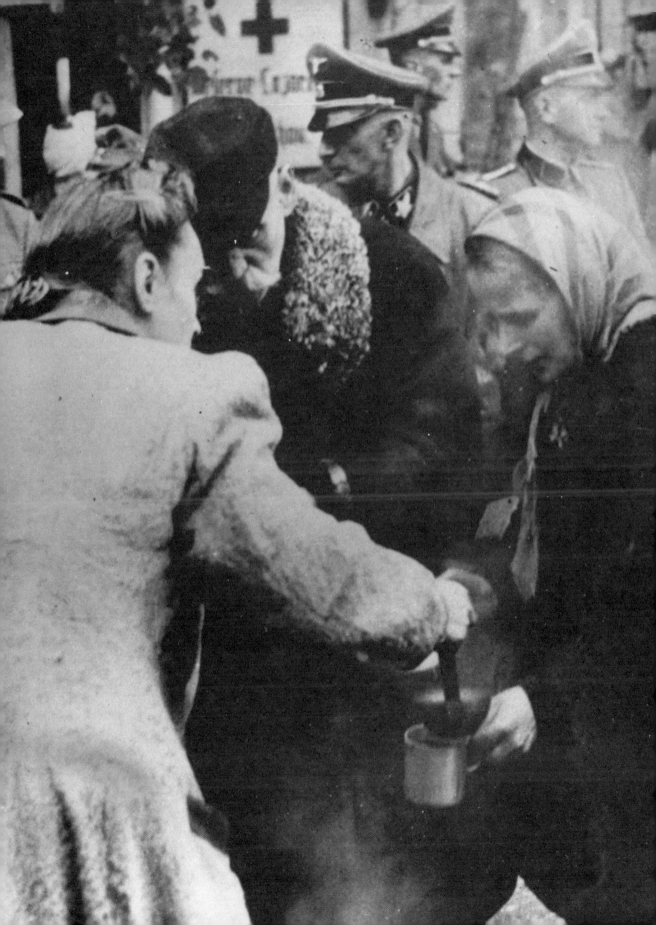

Soviet cavalry on the march in the foothills of the
Carpathian mountains

Artillery in action during the Soviet advance into
Czechoslovakia

left Residents return to their ruined homes on the day of Warsaw's liberation from its Nazi occupiers

above Soviet infantry march through Cracow, the next major Polish city to be liberated after Warsaw

Freedom at last for prisoners in the Maidanek
concentration camp, Poland

Polish villagers share a drink with Soviet soldiers

above Soviet troops welcomed by cheering Bulgarians

right partisans of Tito's Yugoslav Army

left Czechoslovak soldiers erect a new frontier post
on the Dukla Pass – the pre-war frontier

above Prague citizens celebrate the arrival of their
Soviet liberators

Soviet rockets firing at Nazi strongholds during the
siege of Budapest

The aftermath: central Budapest after the German
surrender in February 1945

THE STRAGGLER

'I was never a Nazi at heart'

The Fall of Germany

In February 1945 the task for the Western Allies was to cross the Roer, Our and Saar rivers and reach the Rhine. By 21 February, Goch, Cleve and Calcar were in British and Canadian hands. The US 9th Army threw bridges across the Roer opposite Mönchen Gladbach, which they took on 1 March. Five days later Cologne was in American hands and on 7 March, to the astonishment of the Allies and to Hitler's inexpressible fury, the Remagen Bridge over the Rhine had been taken, apparently undamaged, by the US 1st Army. During the days which followed, auxiliary bridges were thrown across the Rhine, both up- and down-stream from Remagen.

This was fortunate, since on the 17th the bridge at Remagen fell sideways into the Rhine – taking 28 US engineers to their deaths. It had been weakened by German demolition attempts, bombing attacks and thousands of infantry boots and hundreds of heavily loaded vehicles.

On the night of 23 March 1945 Field Marshal Montgomery's 21st Army Group began moving across the Rhine on a broad front. Under massed artillery fire, the first troops crossed in Amphibious Buffalo personnel carriers and DD Sherman tanks. Air support was on an equally massive scale, and the town of Wesel was hit by RAF heavy bombers only a few hundred yards ahead of the advancing troops. This not only cleared Wesel of the enemy but prevented the Germans from moving through the town to counter-attack.

Two divisions of parachute troops were dropped across the Rhine, almost darkening the sky at times. Gliders followed close behind, landing in the Diersfordter Wald and around Mehr-Hamminkeln, but despite massive pre-crossing air raids some flak sites near the landing points escaped the attention of Allied fighter bombers. Offering fierce resistance before being overrun, they shot down or damaged about a quarter of the gliders. Their efforts were futile, however, and the paratroopers and troops that had made the river crossings were able to join up, often well in advance of the anticipated times. By nightfall the Rhine bridgeheads were secure, the 21st Army Group was forging ahead, and despite some local German counterattacks the British and Canadians were across the river to stay.

Further to the south, the Americans were also on the east bank. The day before Montgomery's operation, an assault regiment from Patton's 3rd Army crossed south of Mainz between Nierstein and Oppenheim. By the evening of 23 March the entire 5th Division was over, a bridgehead formed and awaiting the arrival of an armoured division already on the west bank. During the next few days more crossings were made, and by the end of the month Darmstadt and Wiesbaden were in US hands. Armoured columns were driving for Frankfurt-am-Main, and further south the French had put an Algerian division across near Germersheim.

A huge Allied bridgehead stretched from Bonn down to Mannheim, from which would be launched the last Western offensive designed to meet the Soviets on the Elbe and split Germany in two. The main objective for the US 12th Army Group would be the industrial region of Leipzig and Dresden. To the north, the Anglo-Canadian-US 21st Army Group was to drive north towards Hamburg, the Canadians clearing Holland of the enemy and then driving along the coast through Emden and Wilhelmshaven. The US 9th Army was to curve around the Ruhr to meet the US 1st Army at Lippstadt, thus encircling Generalfeldmarschall Walter Model's Army Group 'B' in the Ruhr. After Hamburg the British would close up to the Elbe down as far as Magdeburg, and send other forces up into Schleswig-Holstein and the Baltic.

By the end of March the Rhine from the Channel to the Swiss border was in Allied hands. The Allies were only 485 kilometres from Berlin. Montgomery wanted his 21st Army Group to strike for Berlin, but Eisenhower, sticking to his broad-front strategy and solidly supported by Roosevelt, felt that the German capital was within easier reach of the Soviets.

Stalin informed Marshals Georgi Zhukov and Ivan Koniev on 1 April that the Western Allies were planning to strike for Berlin before the Red Army, but that they were to beat Montgomery to the city. They had planned to attack in early May, but would accelerate all preparations and be ready to move well before the Anglo-Americans could get themselves solidly inside German territory. When the Red Army's final offensive was launched its aims were simple. Advance to the Elbe, annihilate all organized German resistance, and capture Berlin. Zhukov and Koniev had some 1,640,000 men with 6,300 tanks, 41,600 guns and mortars, and 8,400 tactical aircraft in three air armies.

In the face of this overwhelming force, Germany's final defence consisted of seven Panzer and 65 infantry divisions in some sort of order, together with 100 or so independent battalions full of the very young, the old and the sick.

At dawn on 16 April a tremendous artillery and air bombardment opened all along the Oder and Neisse rivers, and out of the Soviet bridgeheads stormed the first waves of shock troops. The German units may have been hastily scraped together, but they could still fight like cornered rats. It took Zhukov two days to smash through some 6.5 kilometres to reach the Seelow Heights in the north – and at that point they had seen no sign of a crack in the German defences despite huge casualties on both sides.

Koniev's shock troops, however, were not so strongly opposed and they advanced 13 kilometres the first day. On the 18th Koniev ordered two tank armies to fight their way to the northwest, into Berlin. Perhaps inspired by competition, Zhukov now drove his infantry and tank armies forward, and by the following day had advanced 30 kilometres on a front almost 65 kilometres wide. The German 9th Army, with no fuel to move, found itself in the way of the steamroller and was annihilated. On 21 April General Chuikov reported that his 8th Guards Army, which had fought all the way across eastern Europe from Stalingrad, was in Berlin's southeastern suburbs.

Leaving the two tank armies fighting for Berlin, the bulk of Koniev's forces now pushed towards the Elbe. On 25 April they linked up with one of Zhukov's guards tank armies which had come around the north of Berlin. Germany's capital and its 200,000-man garrison were surrounded. On the same day units of the 5th Guards Army reached the Elbe at Torgau and within minutes were exchanging drinks, hats, buttons and photographs with Americans of the US 1st Army, splitting Germany in two.

On 1 May Chuikov, now well inside the Berlin city centre, was approached by four officers carrying white flags. Generaloberst Hans Krebs, the Chief of the German General Staff, wished to negotiate the surrender of the city. The first moves towards ending the European war had been made.

Berlin surrendered unconditionally on the 2nd. Two days later Field Marshal Montgomery took the surrender of all German forces in the north – and on 7 May the 'Unconditional surrender of Germany to the Western Allies and to Russia' was agreed. The instrument was signed by General Jodl for the defeated, and Generals Bedell Smith and Suslaparov for the victors, General Sevez also signing for France. A second ceremony took place in Berlin the following day. The war in Europe was at an end.

Hitler, however, did not live to see it. He had committed suicide on 30 April, having first married and then poisoned his mistress Eva Braun, made a will leaving the leadership of his country to Admiral Doenitz, spoken briefly to every member of his personal staff – and poisoned his dog. Afterwards, the bodies of all three were burned.

The Final Months of the War

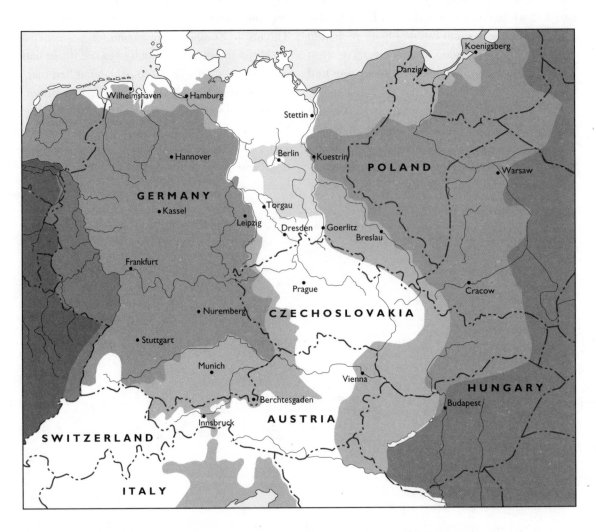

Key: US/British front lines from the west
- US/British front line 16 January 1945
- US/British front line 28 March 1945
- US/British front line 25 April 1945
- US/British front line 7 May 1945

Key: Soviet front lines from the east
- Soviet front line 12 January 1945
- Soviet front line 8 February 1945
- Soviet front line 15 April 1945
- Soviet front line 25 April 1945

Across the Rhine, US paratroopers continue to
advance after linking up with ground forces

British soldiers fight their way from house to house

This German town has fallen into the hands of the
famous British 6th Airborne Division

US infantry sweep across northern Germany towards
Brunswick

The Allied advance was supported by a constant
artillery bombardment of German positions

left The US 76th Tank Battalion moves into what is
left of the old walled city of Nuremberg

below Jubilant Allied troops march into
Saarbrücken

above GIs in Saarbrücken enjoy a little fun at the Führer's expense

right A British airman hangs out his washing on the Siegfried Line

Meanwhile, grim fighting continues as Soviet troops fight their way into the outskirts of Vienna

To Berlin!

left A Russian tank loaded with infantrymen
crosses the river Spree in the drive towards Berlin

above Of the thousands of German prisoners
captured by the Russians, few would ever see
their homes again

The end of the Thousand-Year Reich: German civilians pick their way through the rubble **left** while a Soviet tank sits menacingly by the shattered remnants of the Brandenburg Gate **below**

below The Soviet Union's greatest general, Marshal Zhukov, the architect of every major victory from Moscow to Berlin, seen here on the steps of the Reichstag

above The confidence of the Soviet conquerors
contrasts with the anxiety on the faces of the
German women behind them

left US and Soviet troops enjoying a song on a Russian tank after the link-up on the Elbe

above This 14-year-old German, taken prisoner by the Americans, is clearly happy that for him the war is over

Victory and defeat: **left** the Soviet flag is hoisted
onto the Reichstag building and **below** Zhukov
signs the official German surrender on 8 May

THE PRICE OF FLAGS

'Whatever I pay, it will have cost me more than anything I have ever bought before.'

Victory in Europe

The news of Germany's surrender, although long expected, was an occasion of wild rejoicing. In Britain, years of drabness and belt-tightening were forgotten as an entire nation took to the streets. On 8 May, it was standing room only in the centre of London as Trafalgar Square, Whitehall and the Mall were packed with a seething mass of humanity.

At three pm, Winston Churchill addressed the nation, the radio broadcast being relayed to the people in the streets via loudspeakers. Although Japan was still to be conquered, he said, the war in Europe would end at midnight.

Massed in front of Buckingham Palace, the crowds began to chant: 'We want the King! We want the King!' The royal family appeared on the balcony to roars from the crowd, the first of eight such appearances. As night fell, and the crowds grew ever larger, the biggest cheer of all arose when the King and Queen were joined on the balcony by Churchill. Among the cheering throng were the young Princesses Elizabeth and Margaret, who had sneaked out, escorted by Guards officers, to join the fun.

Hundreds of thousands of people began to celebrate. Licensing laws had been relaxed on this one occasion, and normal British reserve went by the board as strangers hugged and kissed, danced and sang. There were uniforms everywhere – British and American, Free French and Polish, Czech and Dutch, and every service-man seemed to have a pretty girl on his arm.

Similar scenes were taking place all over the world. Crowds thronged Times Square in New York and the Champs Elysées in Paris. In Brussels the celebrations matched the wild joy at the city's liberation the previous autumn.

Among the armies which had fought the final battles, celebrations were more muted, though no less heartfelt. On the Elbe river western and eastern allies met in friendship, a friendship which tragically was not to last as new suspicions and rivalries took shape in post-war Europe and the world.

But there were few celebrations in Germany. Its citizens dug among the ruins of the Thousand-Year Reich, searching for food and trying to prepare some sort of shelter for the coming winter. And as evidence emerged of Nazi inhumanity in the shape of the concentration and extermination camps, there was little sympathy amongst the occupying troops for a people who had allowed such horrors to happen. A hunt began for those responsible. Surviving Nazi leaders had been taken into custody, although some, like Himmler and Goebbels, had followed their demonic leader and committed suicide. A tribunal was set up by the victorious powers to try the Nazis for crimes against humanity and, if necessary, to punish them.

In France, the collaborationist leaders of the Vichy regime were also put on trial. Pierre Laval, a willing tool of the Nazis, had given himself up to the Americans in the hope of lenient treatment, but had been handed over to his country-men. The senile Marshal Pétain, the First World War hero who had been the Vichy figurehead, was also reviled

But all this was to come. For the moment, people were simply glad that the war was over. All too soon, however, the celebrations gave way to a stark reality. The blackout in Britain might have ceased in June, but the lights shone stark on a country which had just about exhausted itself in the prosecution of the war. The great outburst of celebration gave way to a mind-numbing fatigue, as well as relief that life could go on more normally.

The need for a change was reflected in the General Election of 1945. Winston Churchill, who had led the country from the darkest hours of 1940 to ultimate victory in 1945, was defeated in Parliament and his Coalition government resigned. With the bulk of the war over, national unity was no longer seen as essential and party politics returned. In the ensuing General Election in July, the nation declared that it was time to look ahead, and Churchill was voted out of office in a landslide victory by Clement Attlee's Labour Party.

The following month, the war in Japan came to an end when atom bombs were dropped on Hiroshima and Nagasaki. The Second World War was finally over.

In America, President Roosevelt had not lived to see the triumph. He had died in April, to be succeeded by the no-nonsense son of a Mississippi farmer named Harry S. Truman.

Only in the USSR was there any continuity. Stalin had been thinking about the post-war map of Europe for years, and while the free world was setting up the United Nations at a conference in San Francisco, he was using the triumphant Red Army to take control of Eastern Europe. The first inklings of the new world order began to take shape at a conference of the major powers held at Potsdam in July, when Stalin brushed aside western demands that free elections be held in Eastern Europe.

The seeds of the Cold War had been sown.

right His first day of peace

'We want the King!'

The royal family, with Winston Churchill, wave to
the crowd from the balcony of Buckingham Palace

left The crowds gather in Trafalgar square to celebrate VE Day

above A vanload of beer passing through Piccadilly Circus has been hijacked by revellers

Victory celebrations in Red Square, Moscow **above**
and New York City **right**

This young Parisian girl looks forward to a future
without war **left** as soldiers and civilians mingle in
the Champs Elysées **below**

left Copenhagen, May 1945: the Danes rejoice in their freedom after five years of German occupation

above 'What shall we do with the drunken sailor?'

left Some of the thousands of people who thronged
the streets of London

above One of the many street parties that took
place all over the country

V for Victory: this children's party says it all